This book belongs to:

....

Tips for Reading and Sharing

I Like Me, I Like You invites children to think independently and feel good about themselves and others. Children will soon get the hang of the catchy repetitive phrasing and want to add their own ideas. It's a great starting point for discussion – and celebration!

Read on to find out how to get the most fun out of this story.

> I'm good at balancing on one leg.

I like . . .

This rhythmic text is just right for reading aloud. Children will want to stop and talk about the text and pictures as you read. Encourage them to act out their own "I likes," and to add to the list of things they like about themselves and enjoy doing. Join in, too!

> I like my brown hair and the pictures I draw.

> I like the clothes I wear.

Point and say

The lively repetitious text and the bold, colorful pictures give clues to help children predict what will come next. Point to the "I likes" and let your child say them. He will enjoy participating and will begin to recognize the written words. Sharing the book in this way will help your child feel that he is becoming a reader.

I like the friends I make.

People talk

This book provides the perfect opportunity to talk about people – their differences, similarities, feelings, and, of course, likes and dislikes. Let your child lead the conversation, then gently bring up ideas yourself. There are lots of positive images to look at and share!

Picture show and tell

The pictures invite comparisons and comments. Images that reflect your child's own experiences can help him make sense of the world. Similarly, seeing something that is not familiar and asking questions about it helps him learn and understand. Encourage your child to point to things that he notices and talk about them.

I can run fast, too.

Enjoy the book and share your child's pleasure in meeting so many children!

Bernice E. Cullinan

Bernice E. Cullinan
Reading Consultant

For Connor, LA
For Chica, Boussó, Giovanni, Francesco, Anna,
Alice, Sofia, Pietro, Stefano, AG

Dorling  Kindersley

LONDON, NEW YORK, SYDNEY, DELHI, PARIS,
MUNICH, and JOHANNESBURG

Published in the United States by
Dorling Kindersley Publishing, Inc.
95 Madison Avenue,
New York, New York 10016

First American Edition, 2001
2 4 6 8 10 9 7 5 3 1

Text copyright © 2001 by Laurence Anholt
Illustrations copyright © 2001 by Adriano Gon

Library of Congress Cataloging-in-Publication Data
Anholt, Laurence.
I Like Me, I Like You / by Laurence Anholt. – 1st American ed.
p. cm. – (Share-a-story)
Summary: Children describe all the things they like about themselves.
ISBN 0-7894-6352-0 (hardcover)
ISBN 0-7894-5617-6 (paperback)
[1. Self-acceptance–Fiction.] I. Title. II. Share-a-story (DK Publishing, Inc.)
PZ7.A58635 Ik 2000 [E]–dc21 99-049699

Color reproduction by Dot Gradations, UK. Printed by Wing King Tong

Acknowledgements:

Reading Consultant: Wendy Cooling **Series Educational Advisor:** Lianna Hodson
Photographer: Steve Gorton **Models:** Ryan Heaton, Cherise Stephenson, Luke and Ivana Silva
U.S. Consultant: Bernice E. Cullinan, Professor of Reading, New York University

see our complete
catalog at
www.dk.com

I Like Me,
I Like You

by Laurence Anholt   illustrated by Adriano Gon

A Dorling Kindersley Book

I like the way I look.
I like the clothes I wear.

I like the way
I can roll my tongue.

I like
the way
I can comb
my hair.

I like the way my freckles look.

I like the way my teeth look when I smile.

I like me.

I like my body. My body is mine.
I eat good things and exercise to make
myself strong. Because I like me.

I don't look like people in magazines or on TV.
I look like myself and I like me.

I like me because I think for myself. I don't follow the crowd. I can stand up tall and hold my head up high.

I take care of myself because I like me.

I brush my teeth.

Because it makes me feel good and I like me.

I like the pictures I paint.

I like the things I make.

I like the castles I build.

I like the books I share. I like me.

I like the dreams I dream.

When I like me I can do
ANYTHING AT ALL.

Yes, I like me

and
I like
you,
too.!

Activities to Enjoy

I f you've enjoyed this story, you
might like to try some of these
simple, fun activities with your child.

I like skipping.

Act it out

Build self-confidence and awareness of others by taking turns to
show each other the things you're good at: running fast, pulling funny
faces, writing your name, counting to ten, telling stories . . . Talk about
the things you're not so good at, too. Perhaps teach each other how to
do something you do well.

I like counting.

We like playing games

Mirror faces

Look in the mirror and talk about what you see. This will
prompt your child to observe details like eye color, freckles, and
hair style. Try making faces to match different
feelings: happy, sad, surprised, angry. Talk
about what makes your child happy, or
angry, or sad. What does he do when he
feels this way?

If you're happy and you know it

Playing games that exercise different parts of your body are great for building physical awareness and self-esteem. Here are some you might know: "Simon Says"; "Mother, May I?;" "Red Light, Green Light"; "If You're Happy".

If You're Happy

If you're happy and you know it, clap your hands.
If you're happy and you know it, clap your hands.
If you're happy and you know it, and you really want to show it,
If you're happy and you know it, clap your hands.

Verse 2
Stamp your feet

Verse 3
Nod your head

Verse 4
Turn around

Verse 4
Shout "We are!"
(Traditional)

A book about me

Encourage your child to draw pictures of his achievements, his friends, and his family. Offer to write captions: "I like my black hair"; "I like my smile"; "I'm good at running". Bind the pictures together to make your own "I Like Me" book that your child can keep on his bookshelf.

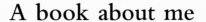

Other Share-a-Story books to enjoy:

Clara and Buster Go Moondancing
   by Dyan Sheldon, illustrated by Caroline Anstey

Mama Tiger, Baba Tiger
   by Juli Mahr, illustrated by Graham Percy

Where's Bitesize?
   by Ian Whybrow, illustrated by Penny Dann

Not Now, Mrs. Wolf!
   by Shen Roddie,
   illustrated by Selina Young

Are You Spring?
   by Caroline Pitcher,
   illustrated by Cliff Wright

The Caterpillar That Roared
   by Michael Lawrence,
   illustrated by Alison Bartlett

Neil's Numberless World
   by Lucy Coats, illustrated by Neal Layton